We played on the swings.
Mom and Dad played too.

We played on the slide.
Mom and Dad played too.

We played on the climbing frame.
Mom and Dad played too.

We played in the pipes.
Mom and Dad played too.

We played on the seats.
Mom and Dad played too.

We played on the see-saw.
Mom and Dad played too.

We played in the tree house.
Mom and Dad played too.

Mom and Dad got so tired we had to take them home early.